Keeping Law Enforcement Connected

Information Technology Needs from State and Local Agencies

John Gordon IV, Brett Andrew Wallace,
Daniel Tremblay, John Hollywood

Sponsored by the National Institute of Justice

RAND Center on Quality Policing

This project was sponsored by the National Institute of Justice and was conducted in the Safety and Justice Program of RAND Justice, Infrastructure, and Environment. The project was supported by Award No. 2010-IJ-CX-K007, awarded by the National Institute of Justice, Office of Justice Programs, U.S. Department of Justice. The opinions, findings, and conclusions or recommendations expressed in this publication are those of the authors and do not necessarily reflect those of the Department of Justice.

Library of Congress Cataloging-in-Publication Data

Gordon, John, 1956-
  Keeping law enforcement connected : information technology needs from state and local agencies /
John Gordon IV, Brett Andrew Wallace, Daniel Tremblay, John Hollywood.
    pages cm
  Includes bibliographical references.
  ISBN 978-0-8330-7806-3 (pbk. : alk. paper)
  1. Law enforcement—Information technology—United States. 2. Law enforcement—United States—Data
processing. 3. Criminal justice, Administration of—Information technology—United States. 4. Criminal justice,
Administration of—United States--Data processing. I. Title.

  HV8141.G67 2012
  363.2068'4—dc23
                                                                                    2012044916

The RAND Corporation is a nonprofit institution that helps improve policy and decisionmaking through research and analysis. RAND's publications do not necessarily reflect the opinions of its research clients and sponsors.

RAND® is a registered trademark.

Published 2012 by the RAND Corporation
1776 Main Street, P.O. Box 2138, Santa Monica, CA 90407-2138
1200 South Hayes Street, Arlington, VA 22202-5050
4570 Fifth Avenue, Suite 600, Pittsburgh, PA 15213-2665
RAND URL: http://www.rand.org/
To order RAND documents or to obtain additional information, contact
Distribution Services: Telephone: (310) 451-7002;
Fax: (310) 451-6915; Email: order@rand.org

Preface

In an effort to assess criminal justice technology needs at the state and local levels, we conducted more than 25 individual and group interviews with criminal justice and law enforcement personnel to arrive at a better understanding of their technology priorities. We also examined the means by which these agencies commonly receive information on technology, including knowledge dissemination at the state and local levels from the National Institute of Justice's (NIJ) National Law Enforcement and Corrections Technology Center (NLECTC). The technical report outlines who we interviewed, what their priorities are regarding information and geospatial technologies and analytic systems, and how they are currently learning about these technologies. It concludes with recommendations to better align investments with agencies' needs and to improve dissemination of information about how to best employ technology.

As is typical for interview and focus-group studies, the analysis in this report is intended to be exploratory, surfacing agencies' needs rather than statistically analyzing their prevalence. Nonetheless, what we heard from the agencies was strongly consistent and more than sufficient to draw preliminary conclusions. Thus, the findings in this report will be of interest to the Department of Justice (DoJ), state and local law enforcement, and technology developers supporting law enforcement.

This research was carried out under the National Law Enforcement Corrections and Technology Center's Information and Geospatial Technology Center of Excellence (IGT CoE). IGT is managed by the Safety and Justice Program of RAND Justice, Infrastructure, and Environment, a division within RAND dedicated to improving policy and decisionmaking in a wide range of policy domains, including civil and criminal justice; infrastructure protection and homeland security; transportation and energy policy; and environmental and natural resources policy.

Questions or comments about this technical report should be sent to the project leader, John Hollywood (johnsh@rand.org). For more information on the Safety and Justice Program, see http://www.rand.org/jie/research/safety-justice.html or contact the director at sj@rand.org.

Contents

Figures and Tables

Figures

Tables

Summary

The National Institute of Justice (NIJ) strives to assist criminal justice practitioners on behalf of the Department of Justice (DoJ) through the scientific research, development, and evaluation of technologies and methods. Given that there are nearly 18,000 state and local law enforcement agencies in the United States, this is a challenge of great complexity, breadth, and depth. Thus, it is crucial to be aware of agencies' technology needs, as well as how they might learn about promising technologies and applications.

This technical report collects a sampling of voices reflective of the law enforcement field on questions related to information and analytic technology needs. It is intended to provide an initial step toward answering questions such as:

- What are the most common and pressing information and analysis technology needs of those serving in the field?
- How can NIJ and its National Law Enforcement and Corrections Technology Center (NLECTC) system best offer assistance?
- How do practitioners currently learn about technology?
- How can NIJ and NLECTC best leverage these modes?
- How successful is NLECTC in interfacing with law enforcement practitioners?

It is important to note that the technology needs expressed by the interviewees draw no distinction between existing systems that they are aware of but cannot afford and new technologies that are not yet developed. Rather, the needs expressed should provide NIJ, other federal providers, and the larger private and academic technology development communities with important insights as to how law enforcement agencies prioritize technology-related issues.

RAND staff conducted more than two dozen group and individual interviews with law enforcement practitioners at the state and local level about their information and analysis technology needs. A concerted effort was made to interview a roughly representative sample of state and local law enforcement organizations in terms of size and geographic location. For example, we talked with a number of very small law enforcement organizations (with as few as four sworn officers), as well as the largest police department in the country—the New York City Police Department. A number of midsized agencies (with a few hundred officers) were also included.

The results of our interviews contained a great deal of commonality regardless of department location or size. We grouped departments by size to illuminate the prevalence of different technology-related issues among small and large departments. Those with more than 100 sworn officers were considered large departments; those with 100 or fewer were considered

Table S.1
Primary Interview Results

Theme	Percentage of Large Departments that Identified Theme	Percentage of Small Departments that Identified Theme	Percentage of All Departments that Identified Theme
DESIRE for improved knowledge management (record management systems [RMS], data exchange)	77	31	54
DESIRE for improved communication infrastructure	62	46	54
DESIRE for cameras/surveillance equipment	54	31	42
DESIRE for low lifecycle cost	69	85	77
INTEROPERABILITY needs to be improved, and the federal government should play a leading role in doing so	69	39	54
PROFESSIONAL associations and conferences are primary sources of technology information	77	77	77
LITTLE or no knowledge of NLECTC	46	77	62

NOTE: Large departments have more than 100 sworn officers; small departments have 100 or fewer.

small. This created an even split of our sample: 13 large departments and 13 small departments. Table S.1 summarizes the themes most commonly heard from participants.

In the area of technology needs, the most prevalent concern expressed by those in the field was for improved knowledge management systems. This desire involved not only the ability to store information in their RMS, but also the ability to disseminate information to those in the department when and where they need it. The second most common desire was for assistance with basic communications infrastructure. Smaller and more rural departments tended to have very limited funds and were therefore incapable of acquiring basic communications equipment, such as radios (whether handheld or vehicle-mounted) and dispatch equipment to the extent needed. Larger departments with more sworn officers had issues due to the proportionally larger budget required to maintain a larger inventory of communication equipment. The third most common desire was for assistance with camera and surveillance systems. Many departments were unable to afford items such as digital in-car cameras or lapel cameras in needed quantities, or they desired a greater number of surveillance cameras in urban areas. Those who did have sufficient surveillance equipment desired greater capabilities, such as increased digital storage or the ability to easily review video via rewinding and fast-forwarding.

Blanketing the technology needs were the issues of interoperability and of cost, specifically in terms of the entire system lifecycle. Small departments often have budgets so limited as to sharply restrict the acquisition of even relatively basic equipment such as simple radios, and 85 percent of departments with 100 or fewer sworn officers identified this issue. Large departments are not spared, as outfitting a much larger number of sworn officers with new equipment carries a proportional increase in cost. Lastly, the multitude of vendors competing to sell their equipment to practitioners often adopt different, and occasionally proprietary, data standards. This becomes a large issue when information must be shared across departments and especially across state boundaries. Those we interviewed consistently expressed a desire for the federal government to push data standards that would alleviate this problem.

The input we received from practitioners illuminated several courses of action that we recommend to address the common concerns laid out by criminal justice practitioners, and to increase the interaction those same practitioners have with NIJ via NLECTC. We recommend that NIJ-funded research include a focus on improving the capability of knowledge management systems, with special attention paid to lifecycle cost. We also recommend a forward-looking study investigating the feasibility and practicality of the federal government leading the development of selected standards for law enforcement records management and information technologies, in conjunction with practitioner and developer communities. This study should build on the significant government-led work on improving information sharing to date, as well as related work by practitioner and vendor associations. In addition, we recommend a focused effort to increase interoperability of RMS data as well as communication systems. To directly address departments' needs to reduce procurement cost, we recommend creation of a repository for federally funded criminal justice software, training, and source code, providing a centralized database for practitioners.

These priorities apply not just to NIJ, but to federal, academic, and industry providers of information and analytic technologies for law enforcement, as well. There needs to be research and development (R&D) not just on technologies, but on the acquisition business that make the full lifecycle costs (direct and indirect) affordable to departments. Further, there needs to be R&D on both the technological and supporting business models to improve the interoperability of the new systems, building on the significant federal and industry work in this area to date.

Lastly, we note that NLECTC is largely unknown among those it is designed to serve. Law enforcement practitioners, who need the technology that NIJ attempts to assist them with, showed little familiarity with NLECTC or other NIJ-led efforts to provide outreach to the field. A clear insight from the interviews was that law enforcement practitioners make extensive use of professional associations (e.g., Police Chiefs and Sheriffs Associations) to obtain information on new technologies and for information sharing. Indeed, this reliance on the law enforcement associations for information was such a strong, common insight that its importance is hard to overstate. We recommend that NIJ—as well as other federal agencies and academic and commercial developers—leverage these associations, such as the International Association of Chiefs of Police (IACP), the National Sheriffs' Association (NSA), and the Police Executive Research Forum (PERF) as additional channels to disseminate information and raise awareness of NLECTC and other NIJ technology support efforts.

Acknowledgments

The authors thank Steve Schuetz of the National Institute of Justice for his assistance in helping guide and facilitate this research. There were numerous law enforcement officials at the state and local levels who generously provided time to meet with RAND staff during our interviews. The insights these men and women provided to the research team were invaluable. Additionally, Christine Famega of California State University, San Bernardino, and the authors' colleague Eric Landree contributed vital feedback and ideas critical to the completion of this technical report.

Abbreviations

CoE	Center of Excellence
DoJ	Department of Justice
IACP	International Association of Chiefs of Police
IGT	Information and Geospatial Technology
IT	information technology
LPR	license plate reader
NIJ	National Institute of Justice
NLECTC	National Law Enforcement and Corrections Technology Center
NSA	National Sheriffs' Association
PD	police department
PERF	Police Executive Research Forum
R&D	research and development
RMS	records management systems
TWG	Technology Working Group

CHAPTER ONE

Introduction

Coordinating, unifying, and surveying law enforcement organizations in the United States is an undertaking fraught with difficulties. There are roughly 18,000 state and local police departments (PDs) in the nation, in addition to dozens of federal law enforcement authorities, plus court systems and correctional facilities at the local, state, and federal level.[1] No one governance body sits at the top of them all, many have overlapping jurisdictions, and each is responsible to a different constituency. Indeed, it is worth remembering the original intent of the framers of the Constitution in granting state and local governments their own criminal justice organizations—to resist encroachment from the federal government. Alexander Hamilton's "Federalist 17" explains why the balance of power rests with the states in criminal justice:

> There is one transcendent advantage belonging to the province of the State governments
> . . . the ordinary administration of criminal and civil justice. This, of all others, is the most
> powerful, most universal, and most attractive source of popular obedience and attachment
> . . . as to render them at all times a complete counterpoise, and, not infrequently, dangerous
> rivals to the power of the Union (Hamilton, 1787).

Federal criminal justice programs, such as the National Institute of Justice (NIJ) and its National Law Enforcement and Corrections Technology Center (NLECTC) system, are thus placed in a vexing situation: They are designed to assist thousands of state and local criminal justice organizations but have no hierarchical authority or structure in place to control or coordinate those organizations' actions. For NIJ and other federal agencies to achieve their missions, they must be able reach out to law enforcement agencies across the country, both to collect information on which technology needs are most pressing and to disseminate information on what technology solutions might be most useful. This report is intended to take an initial step toward characterizing agencies' needs for information and analytic technologies, as well as identifying mechanisms that show promise for improving NIJ's (and other federal agencies') outreach to state and local agencies.

This report is intended to build on prior studies that examined information technology-related needs at a high level as part of general surveys on law enforcement technology needs (Schwabe, Davis, and Jackson, 2001; Collins et al., 2004; Koper et al., 2009; International Association of Chiefs of Police, 2012; Reaves, 2010). As will be discussed, our findings are broadly consistent with the findings of the earlier studies, with our results providing more detail specifically on information and analytic needs. It is also intended to help guide the devel-

---

[1] As of 2008, the official U.S. government census reported 17,985 agencies (Reaves, 2011).

opment of questions about information and analytic technology needs on future broad-based surveys of law enforcement.

The RAND Corporation was given the status of the NLECTC Center of Excellence (CoE) for Information and Geospatial Technology (IGT) in 2011. Central to this role is a strategic planning effort that examines the state of technology and research within four portfolios: Information-Led Policing, Geospatial Technologies, Operations Research, and Modeling and Simulation. As an input to this strategic assessment, RAND CoE staff set up a robust liaison and outreach program that involved interviewing members of a broad range of criminal justice agencies of different sizes and jurisdictions, attending law enforcement conferences, conducting visits to NIJ-funded projects, and coordinating the efforts of four Technology Working Groups (TWGs). Using these inputs, this technical report is intended to

- provide an initial characterization of state and local criminal justice information technology (IT) and analysis technology needs and priorities for NIJ, as well as federal, academic, and commercial technology providers to law enforcement
- assess NIJ and NLECTC's current outreach activities to state and local law enforcement and recommend possible avenues to improve knowledge dissemination[2]
- recommend practical ways to guide research funded by NIJ so it better aligns with law enforcement practitioner needs.

---

[2]   NIJ and NLECTC's current outreach activities are discussed in the appendix.

CHAPTER TWO

Research Methodology

The results of this report are derived from a qualitative analysis of focus groups and interviews with the criminal justice community conducted by RAND's liaison and outreach staff. As is typical for qualitative analysis studies (see, for example, Grudens-Shuck, Allen, and Larson, 2004), the results are intended to surface agencies' information and analytic technology needs.[1] As will be seen, the results were consistent enough across agencies to make initial assessments of prevalence, as well.

Interviews

Table 2.1 lists the organizations that participated in an interview, along with their respective state and the number of sworn officers employed. We interviewed representatives from 26 organizations in separate sessions—a significantly higher number than the four to six groups typical for qualitative analysis studies (see, for example, National Oceanic and Atmospheric Administration Coastal Services Center, 2009, and Groups Plus, 2008). To get input from a sample of agencies representative of the range of departments in the United States, we interviewed small, medium, and large organizations, from those with as few as four sworn officers to those with thousands. Multiple types of jurisdictions were also represented, including local, county, state, university, and federal/state interagency.

Results will be displayed in terms of department size. "Large" departments belong to the biggest 50 percent of departments we interviewed in terms of sworn officers, totaling 13 departments all employing more than 100 sworn officers. "Small" departments comprise the bottom 50 percent of departments in terms of sworn officers. This group also consists of 13 departments, all with 100 or fewer sworn officers.

Geographically, 15 of the nation's 50 states were represented, plus the District of Columbia. Jurisdictionally, approximately 77 percent of the participants were local police organizations as opposed to state or other types, which is a proportion comparable to the 70 percent distribution reflected in the nationwide data reported in the most recent law enforcement census results from the Department of Justice (DoJ).[2]

Participating agencies were recruited through a variety of methods. Many participants were recruited from the NIJ Technology Institute in Annapolis, a five-day NIJ-sponsored conference with 30 local law enforcement officials from departments that employed less than 50 sworn officers. Other participants were recruited during the Spring 2011 Conference

---

[1] This differs from large-sample surveys, which would be used to statistically assess the prevalence of the needs.

[2] As of 2008, the official U.S. government census was 17,985 agencies (Reaves, 2011).

Table 2.1
List of Departments Interviewed

Department	State	Total Sworn
Akron PD	OH	430
Arcadia PD	CA	68
Beverly Hills PD	CA	100
California Highway Patrol	CA	7,500
Charleston PD	SC	412
Chicago PD	IL	13,500
Elizabeth PD	CO	5
Dallas PD	TX	3,500
Detroit PD	MI	2,845
The George Washington University PD	DC	100
High Springs PD	FL	16
Holden PD	MA	24
La Vista PD	NE	34
Inglewood PD	CA	189
Lancaster County Sheriff	NE	76
Lincoln PD	NE	317
Nebraska State Patrol	NE	488
New York PD	NY	35,386
Pasadena PD	CA	244
Philadelphia PD	PA	6,700
Princeton Borough PD	NJ	30
Seahawk Interagency Operations Center	SC	30
Stronghurst PD	IL	4
Truth or Consequences PD	NM	15
University Park PD	TX	39
Virginia State Police	VA	2,008

of the International Association of Chiefs of Police (IACP) Law Enforcement Information Management. Finally, some departments were recruited through standing relationships with RAND or RAND researchers.

Each interview lasted an hour or two, and group size ranged from one to eight participants. To get a diverse sample of perspectives, interviews were conducted with sergeants, analysts, and administrative officers, in addition to chiefs, sheriffs, and police commissioners. We have included a list of the ranks and titles of the various officers and civilians who participated in interviews.

Job Titles of Individuals Interviewed

Police Chief
Police Commissioner
Sheriff
Colonel
Deputy Chief, Strategic Deployment Bureau
Deputy Chief, Support Services
Deputy Chief, Technical Services Bureau
Assistant Chief
Deputy Commissioner, Field Operations
Deputy Commissioner, Organizational Support Services
Assistant Commissioner
Lieutenant Colonel
Lieutenant Colonel, Director of Administrative and Support Services
Chief Administrative Officer
Director, Predictive Analytics
Director, Office of Performance Management and Internal Controls
Deputy Inspector
Assistant Director, IT
Commander, Criminal Intelligence
Captain
Captain, Technology Infrastructure
Captain, Investigation Bureau
Captain, Investigative Services
Lieutenant
Lieutenant, Office of the Academy
Lieutenant, High Tech Crimes Division
Lieutenant, Task Force Agent
First Sergeant, Technical Support
Sergeant
Sergeant, Research and Development (R&D), Planning & Crime Analysis
Sergeant, Field Intelligence Unit Supervisor
Surveillance Agent
Geospatial Analyst
Crime Analyst
Lead Management Analyst
System Programmer
IT Manager
Public Safety GIS Program Manager
Planning and Research Manager
Administrative Officer

Questions

During the interviews, we used a series of semi-structured questions asking respondents to describe their information and analysis technology needs, their current awareness of NLECTC's outreach efforts, and their current means for learning about new technologies. The following were the key questions:

- Have you ever heard of the National Law Enforcement and Corrections Technology Center, or NLECTC? If so, what aspects of NLECTC outreach are you aware of? Do you use JUSTNET? Have you heard of *TechBeat*? [3] Do you have any NIJ grants?
- What is the process you currently use to communicate your law enforcement technology needs? To whom (what agency) do your requests and needs go? How do you currently find out about newly available technologies and systems?
- If you had the opportunity to communicate law enforcement technology needs to NIJ, what do you think the best way to do that would be, from your organization's perspective?
- We'd like you to think about what you and the agency do during both routine operations and during a major incident. As you think about these, can you tell the situations where you most wish you had some sort of information or tool that would make your life easier? We want to identify a "hot list" of the most pressing unmet needs for IT, analysis, and training tools.
- What is a high-level description of where your department/office is in terms of the following systems and technologies:
  - geospatial analysis
  - predictive policing
  - deployed systems (cameras/license plate reader [LPR]/mobiles)
  - data and networking infrastructure
  - operations research (analytic models for decision support)
  - modeling and simulation
  - training systems (virtual reality or gaming)?
- Are there any other ways in which your department uses data to support your strategic planning, tactical operations, or evaluation that we are leaving out?
- Out of the systems/technology you mentioned:
  - Which of them work well? Which don't?
  - What are the most important areas for improvement, and where do you think your largest capability gaps are?
  - How do you think you compare to other departments?
  - Have you had problems with implementation and lifecycle costs?
- Do you have any lessons learned to share about your experiences with acquiring these systems from technology vendors?
- Do you have your own R&D budget for these types of technologies? How much is it?

---

[3] The Justice Technology Information Network, or JUSTNET, is NLECTC's public website. *TechBeat* is NLECTC's quarterly news magazine. More information is available in the appendix.

Coding

We prepared detailed minutes from each session. We then analyzed each set of minutes, identifying and marking ("coding") technology needs and methods for learning about technology stated during each session.[4] We also coded the participants' stated awareness of NLECTC's existing outreach activities. In some cases, participants volunteered statements on what they felt NIJ or the federal government's role should be in assisting state and local agencies with technology; we also coded these statements. We then calculated the percentages of agencies making similar statements, as measured by the presence of codes; these percentages provide very preliminary estimates of prevalence. Chapter Three captures the results of this analysis, providing numerical results, detailed discussions of the themes that emerged from the sessions, and exemplar quotes.

Limitations

The methodology utilized here has its limitations. First, only a few dozen law enforcement organizations were interviewed out of the thousands nationwide; the results should be considered preliminary, surfacing needs rather than precisely assessing their prevalence. That said, we believe the results showed enough consistency across agencies to make some preliminary assessments of the commonality regarding needs and mechanisms for learning about technologies. Second, this study only interviewed law enforcement agencies. Other criminal justice entities, including courts and corrections institutions, are not represented. Third, we used snowball sampling to recruit participants, using prior relationships and technology conferences. As noted, we made an effort to interview a sample of agencies reflective of U.S. law enforcement as a whole; however, the fact that many participants were recruited from technology conferences may lead to the following biases:

- Participating agencies may have a higher level of technological sophistication than the norm, being more aware of cutting-edge information and analysis technologies and their uses.
- Participating agencies may have a higher level of awareness of NIJ's and NLECTC's outreach activities than the norm. (The Rural Technology Institute, in particular, was sponsored by NLECTC.)

Fourth, interviewees answered questions extemporaneously, rather than engaging in any rigorous or systemic assessment of departmental needs. Participants were free to describe existing capabilities that they were unable to procure or maintain, as well as technology that may not yet exist. They were not asked to discern. Thus, we were able to capture a broad range of responses related to technology needs. As noted, this research is intended to be an initial step in characterizing departments' technology needs and learning mechanisms. We make recommendations for further research in the conclusions in Chapter Four.

---

[4] For more information on qualitative analysis of interview and focus group reports, focusing on coding common themes within the reports, see, e.g., Zhang and Wildemuth, 2009.

CHAPTER THREE

Results

Three main themes became apparent from the interview and focus group results:

- The most-cited technology priorities were for basic IT knowledge management systems (notably records management systems [RMS]), basic communications infrastructure, and, to a lesser extent, camera systems.
- There is a strong and consistent need to address procurement issues, especially reducing the end-to-end lifecycle costs of these major systems and improving the interoperability of IT systems. Further, respondents commonly stated that NIJ should play a leading role in improving interoperability.
- Respondents consistently relied heavily on law enforcement associations (e.g., police chiefs' associations) to gain information on new technologies and to share information. Vendors were also reported as a significant source. In contrast, few agencies reported significant awareness of NLECTC's current activities.

The prevalence of these themes across the participating agencies is reported in Table 3.1 and is discussed in more detail below.

These themes encapsulate the most common technology-related needs of participating organizations. The next most common theme was the desire for the federal government to serve as a clearinghouse for law enforcement equipment information. Four of 26 interviewees, or 15 percent, identified this theme. (We do identify this as a recommendation; see Chapter Four.)

Technology Priorities

As previously mentioned, interviewees were asked a number of semi-structured questions and encouraged to elaborate on the technology-related issues with the most impact. As such, the technology priorities described encompassed a number of areas, including the inability to procure equipment, the desire for greater capabilities for equipment they already possessed, or the wish for certain equipment or functionality that had not yet been developed. Within this framework, interview participants described their most pressing needs. Two themes emerged: (1) knowledge management and (2) basic communications infrastructure. Both of these topics were noted priorities for 54 percent of all departments we interviewed, regardless of size. Desires for cameras and surveillance systems followed closely behind as a third theme.

Knowledge management. Primarily, respondents wanted better knowledge management systems, with 77 percent of large departments and 31 percent of small ones identifying

Table 3.1
Primary Interview Results

Theme	Percentage of Large Departments that Identified Theme	Percentage of Small Departments that Identified Theme	Percentage of All Departments that Identified Theme
Desire for improved knowledge management (RMS, data exchange)	77	31	54
Desire for improved communication infrastructure	62	46	54
Desire for cameras/surveillance equipment	54	31	42
Desire for low lifecycle cost	69	85	77
Interoperability needs to be improved and the federal government should play a leading role in doing so	69	39	54
Professional associations and conferences are primary sources of technology information	77	77	77
Little or no knowledge of NLECTC	46	77	62

NOTE: Large departments have more than 100 sworn officers; small departments have 100 or fewer.

this priority. Improved knowledge management systems involve getting the right information to the right people at the right time—including within the department, to the officers in the field, and with other departments. Specifically, the most common answer to this question was better RMS. Departments happy with their RMS either had new ones or had the programming staff to constantly modify and update their system in-house. Those respondents had drastically fewer capability gaps because their RMS underpinned all of their department's IT. But knowledge management issues were a priority even for departments that were happy with their RMS, although their concerns were more tactical. Priority capabilities of this type included the ability to share telephone or LPR data between departments, to have greater automated data population capabilities when writing reports, or to push information such as suspect photos, maps, and camera views to officers in the field. Other knowledge management

---

Respondents' Comments on Knowledge Management

"The ability to share knowledge across the department is key. What is going on at a very local level, who is working, who is where? Just the ability to share knowledge. Having collaborative software . . . Nobody really knows what is in every box or in every system right now: You don't know what is in production or in staging."

"Everything is underpinned by our RMS."

"Create an open system for RMS. RMS for medium and small agencies are killing their budgets."

"Records and information. That is my no. 1 priority."

Respondents' Comments on Communications Infrastructure

"Mobile connectivity is a priority."

"We don't have enough AirCards . . . downloading is killing us."

"Where we are hurting is in capacity. The state doesn't have enough money to pay for all of that bandwidth."

---

issues that were commonly mentioned were the need for a federated search capability, data warehousing, and data standards.

Basic communications infrastructure. The second common theme was the need for a solid and reliable basic communications infrastructure. CoE staff expected this issue to mostly be applicable to small and rural departments due to their less sophisticated technologies, larger patrol areas with fewer officers, and spotty cell-tower coverage in rural areas, and the issue was identified by 62 percent of small departments. Some smaller departments did not have sufficient funding to establish a modern communications network capable of quickly relaying information. But larger departments also expressed issues with network bandwidth and connectivity problems, although their problems related to the high cost of upgrading hardware for a large number of officers and vehicles, and the fact that a department's size is directly proportional to its required bandwidth capacity. Among large departments, 46 percent identified communications infrastructure as a technology-related issue. A majority of departments expressed a desire for faster Internet access, greater bandwidth, more AirCards, better cell phone service, or upgraded radios that are interoperable with other jurisdictions.

Cameras and surveillance systems. Finally, the most frequent second-tier priority clustered around cameras and surveillance systems, which was expressed by approximately 54 percent of large departments and 31 percent of small ones. Officers frequently indicated they would like to have lapel cameras, digital in-car cameras, and more urban surveillance cameras. Even those departments that had sophisticated camera capabilities expressed a desire to have them improved with better video data storage, the ability to rewind and fast-forward, and the ability to get access to school district cameras.

Respondents' Comments on Surveillance Systems

"As for priorities, we would like fully comprehensive use of cameras, and to be able to pull up the feed and see those in multiple views, to be able to rewind, and get interfaces and understanding with what is going on with every business on certain streets. We want to be able to take over a hospital's camera system, for example; . . . we also want rapidly deployable cameras . . . that can be put out at any scene immediately."

"Another priority would be lapel cameras for officers to have on their uniforms."

"The only reason we don't have in-car cameras is because of our budget."

Procurement Needs

Lifecycle cost. First, the emphasis was on systems that could be procured for a low cost. Cost was specifically singled out as a prohibitive factor to meeting technology needs by 69 percent of the large departments interviewed and an overwhelming 85 percent of the small departments. Officers would prefer to have a medium-quality, low-cost system that gets the job done over the fanciest, state-of-the-art system that is extremely expensive. The procurement cycle for replacing hardware at police departments is often around seven years, but the state of technology is accelerating so rapidly that systems are usually out of date within three to five years. That quick cycle makes low-cost procurements essential. But direct up-front costs are only part of the cost equation. Even when departments receive technology as the result of a grant, there is the issue of sustainability. Maintenance fees, training costs, and licensing costs over the lifecycle of a system can often be more expensive than the up-front cost of purchasing it. Although this is a bigger problem for some departments than others, all were acutely aware of the costs and difficulties of sustaining procured systems.

Interoperability and a proposed leading role for the Department of Justice. Many departments purchase technology through a co-op, or with their adjoining county or municipal jurisdictions. Or they purchase a system because the county, the state, or a larger neighboring jurisdiction already has that system, and the department wants theirs to be interoperable. Regardless of the purchasing process, many departments want to ensure interoperability and thus make decisions about what systems to purchase based on what their neighbors have.

Respondents' Comments on Lifecycle Costs

"All the maintenance costs are too high. We get a grant in, [but] in the out years, it is all on the city."

"Having all our own systems since the late 90s, we are up to $500,000 a year now that we save because we no longer need to support paying maintenance fees to outside software developers."

"We drill vendors to make sure technology can ensure return on investment over ten years. Even when systems become obsolete after a few years, we still have to run it. Technology turns over in three to five years. And with the state of the economy, we can't keep up with that."

Interoperability was an issue for 69 percent of large departments and 39 percent of small departments. Agency officials complained about the lack of standards among the vendors, particularly for information and communications systems. It was noted by a number of police chiefs that even within their own state there could be lack of law enforcement IT standards to the point that it inhibited the ability to quickly share data and information.

Many interviewees expressed their attitudes regarding what the federal government's role should be and how it should channel its efforts. Overwhelmingly, law enforcement officials volunteered that the federal government should focus on developing standards for law enforcement technology. For example, officers expressed the desire for the federal government to develop standards for encryption, network security protocols, D-block–based wireless networks, Radio over Internet Protocol, next-generation 911 calls, regionalization data-sharing standards, starting a

---

Respondents' Comments on NIJ's Role

"The main thing for NIJ would be to come up with standards. We need to be interoperable . . . what do you want to get back . . . how is it captured and how can it be sent . . . in what format. Come up with those standards . . . We need universal interoperability."

"[Setting] standards is a legitimate role for the feds . . . come up with standards and if a vendor wants to play in this box, their product ought to meet certain standards. . . . The feds see themselves as a bank rather than the ones that should go in a room and think these things through."

"NIJ should do anything that would enhance existing systems and enhance standards."

"The feds should be a benchmark setter."

---

fusion center, and open-source RMS. Although nobody expressed a desire for DoJ to stop funding criminal justice research, the enthusiasm level for developing industry standards trumped any other envisioned role for DoJ. The consensus was that if DoJ could establish common standards, the vendors would build their equipment to those standards.

Primary Sources of Technology Information

Primary role of associations. The vast majority of the agencies we met with stated that their main source of information on new law enforcement technology was either from sheriffs' or police chiefs' associations and their conferences—such as the IACP, the National Sheriffs' Association (NSA), and the Police Executive Research Forum (PERF)—or directly from law enforcement equipment vendors. None of these entities are federal-level government organizations.

The consistency of the response from state and local law enforcement practitioners regarding the reliance on sheriffs' and police chiefs' associations as their main source of information on new technologies and as information-sharing mechanisms cannot be overstated. Almost 77 percent of interviewees from both large and small departments expressed their use of these associations.

A related theme from the interviews was that vendors who provide law enforcement technologies were another very important source of information for the state and local agencies. Sometimes the local law enforcement officials meet the vendors at conventions, sometimes

---

Respondents' Comments on Associations' Roles

"The associations are almost a de facto standard as an outlet of information."

"Associations are a huge source of info for big-city chiefs, too."

"The annual IACP meeting is also the main way we find out about technology."

"The best way to get information out is through these associations."

---

they are put in contact with a vendor via association networks—while in other cases, vendors approach them directly.

Awareness of NLECTC's efforts. All interviewees were asked if they had heard of NLECTC, and if they were aware of or had used its various means of outreach, including JUSTNET and *TechBeat*. CoE staff reviewed the interview results as a whole and assessed a score for each department. Table 3.2 explains the rating descriptions.

Figure 3.1 displays the distribution of awareness ratings for the participating departments. The vast plurality of the 26 departments reported "No awareness" of NLECTC or JUSTNET. Aggregating the total scores gives an average awareness-level score of 1.5 for large departments and 0.7 for small departments. The overall average score of 1.1 reflects a ranking of "Low." As noted above, rather than learning about new law enforcement technologies from a federal entity, the large majority of the practitioners we interviewed stressed that they get information via the network provided by the sheriffs' and police chiefs' associations, and secondarily from vendors.

Results from Prior Studies

Results from prior studies of law enforcement needs are broadly consistent with our results. Note that these studies largely asked agencies about the prevalence or perceived information technologies at a high level, as part of broad surveys about law enforcement needs in general. Further, given recent advances in (and widespread dissemination of) mobile devices and other electronics, many of the prevalence statistics cited in earlier reports are undoubtedly much lower than current figures.

Schwabe, Davis, and Jackson (2001), in a survey of law enforcement agencies, found that large fractions of local departments had "obsolete or old" radio equipment, administrative/accounting systems, and computers. Several also lacked camera systems and computers in patrol cars.

Collins et al. (2004) surveyed 239 small and rural agencies with fewer than 20 sworn officers; they found comparatively few small departments using technologies such as cameras, digital imaging, global positioning system tracking, and in-car computers.

Koper et al. (2009) surveyed 300 agencies affiliated with the Police Executive Research Foundation and conducted a two-day workshop including representatives from 29 agencies. The top five priority areas they identified were managing service calls, crime analysis and intelligence-led policing, IT technology and database integration, prevention and investiga-

Table 3.2
NLECTC Awareness Rating Descriptions

Rating	Meaning	Possible Examples
0	No awareness	Never heard of NLECTC or JUSTNET
1	Low level of awareness	Has heard of NLECTC or JUSTNET in passing
2	Medium level of awareness	Knows about NLECTC, has been to JUSTNET, gets *TechBeat*
3	High level of awareness	Works with NLECTC, visits JUSTNET frequently, or has received NIJ funding

Figure 3.1
Distribution of NLECTC Awareness

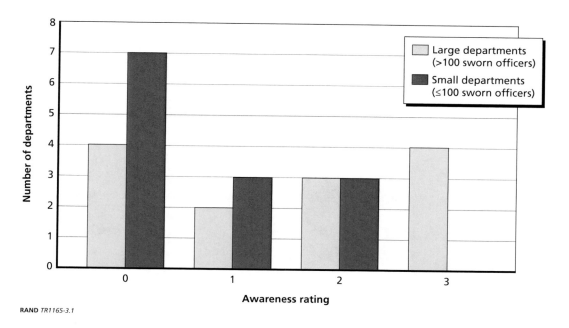

RAND *TR1165-3.1*

tion of street crime, and hiring and retention of officers. The study also named "financial constraints" and "impediments to information sharing" as two of the top seven barriers to technology acquisition.

The International Association of Chiefs of Police (2012) conducted an online survey of 47 agencies; the top technology priorities named by respondents there included mobile data terminals, radios, communications bandwidth, cellular phones, and camera systems of various types.

Finally, Reaves (2010), reporting on the Bureau of Justice Statistics' 2007 Law Enforcement Management and Administrative Statistics survey, found that 79 percent of departments reported using computerized records management, 49 percent reported using computers for dispatch, 59 percent reported using mobile computers in the field, and 66 percent reported using some form of camera system on a regular basis. These statistics represented large increases over the 1997 and 2000 surveys, and lesser increases over the 2003 survey.

CHAPTER FOUR

Recommendations and Conclusions

Summary: Conclusions from the Outreach Sessions

The CoE liaison and outreach team's results offer the following conclusions:

- In making technology investment decisions, NIJ and federal, academic, and commercial technology providers should note that the most frequently reported priorities were to improve access to knowledge management capabilities, specifically RMS, and basic communications infrastructure. While some departments desired improved capabilities, the emphasis from interviewees was primarily on making these technologies more affordable over the lifetime of the equipment. Cameras and surveillance systems are a lower, but still important, priority.
- Value criteria to help shape priority decisions include low direct cost, low lifecycle cost, and interoperability. Participants frequently stated needs to lower lifecycle costs and improve system interoperability.
- Practitioners repeatedly stated that the federal government should play a lead role in setting technology standards. Agency representatives were highly receptive to the government setting technology standards and providing guidance on what systems to purchase. A broad swath of newly evolving technology domains could benefit from federal guidance.
- The most common sources of law enforcement technology information exchange are associations. Conversely, NLECTC currently has low user-community awareness. NLECTC outreach and awareness of the NLECTC system must be improved to ensure that the Center accomplishes its mission of assisting with addressing the technology needs and challenges of state, local, tribal, and federal law enforcement outfits, as well as those of corrections and criminal justice agencies.

Recommendations

Technology Investments

Based on interviews and focus group results, including their desired value criteria, priorities, and need for standards, NIJ and its NLECTC system should focus on several R&D and support needs.

R&D investments should address three priorities. The first is improving internal departmental knowledge management capabilities—specifically for more capable, yet affordable, records management systems. The second is to support departments that share information externally; examples might include solicitations to set standards for open, non-proprietary architectures to integrate criminal justice data between organizations. Third, NIJ should contemplate how R&D investments could go toward best practices for reducing acquisition and lifecycle costs for both basic communications infrastructures and camera surveillance systems, given that these were the second and third most commonly desired capabilities (behind RMS) that police departments are unable to afford.

We emphasize that these priorities are not just for NIJ—they apply equally to those providing technologies to law enforcement agencies, including federal, academic, and industry partners. There needs to be R&D not just on technologies, but on the business models for disseminating technologies that make the full lifecycle costs (direct and indirect) affordable to departments. Regionalization, licensing, and shared service models are some possible frameworks that have been proposed as answers to cost. Further, there needs to be R&D on both the technological and supporting business models to improve the interoperability of the new systems. These efforts should build on the significant work on information sharing by groups such as the Global Justice Information Sharing Initiative and the National Information Exchange Model Program Management Office, as well as by practitioner associations (IACP, 2012) and industry (Integrated Justice Information Systems Institute, 2010).

Additionally, attention should be paid not just to direct R&D but also to the facilitation of R&D and subsequent dissemination in the criminal justice community. Following up on stated needs to reduce lifecycle costs, it would be of high value to disseminate free (or very inexpensive) tools and training to law enforcement; as noted, this was an idea named by four responding agencies. We recommend that NIJ develop and maintain a federal repository containing federally funded software packages, source code, and training materials of use to law enforcement. Currently, there is no central location to store these materials and make them available to practitioners. Further, NIJ and its federal partners should explore areas in which it would be appropriate for the federal government to lead the development of standards for criminal justice technology and systems, working with practitioner and industry partners. These would be forward-looking studies to assess technology trends in law enforcement, determine which domains could feasibly have an industry standard, and emulate past successes in body armor standardization, testing, and evaluation. All of the preceding recommendations are summarized in Table 4.1.

Given these results, several actions can be taken to both improve NLECTC's processes for outreach, including gathering input from criminal justice practitioners to optimize NIJ's

Table 4.1
R&D and R&D Support Needs

Category	Possible Examples
R&D	Improving RMS capabilities and reducing their costs
R&D	Interoperability and integration among criminal justice data systems
R&D	Best practices to decrease costs and effectively implement basic communications infrastructure
R&D	Best practices to decrease costs and effectively implement camera and surveillance systems
R&D Support	Develop standards for emerging law enforcement technology trends
R&D Support	Federal repository for law enforcement software, source code, and training packages

investment portfolio. But first, NIJ must also set priorities within its R&D portfolio that align with practitioner needs. Otherwise, increasing outreach and awareness becomes a moot point if NLECTC offers no services useful to criminal justice practitioners.

Outreach and Dissemination

When asked what the best mechanism would be for NIJ to disseminate information and make the criminal justice community aware of NLECTC resources, the overwhelming response was to utilize professional associations, as previously discussed. These include the IACP, NSA, PERF, the International Association of Campus Law Enforcement Administrators, the International Association of Crime Analysts, the American Correctional Association, and the American Jail Association, to name a few. Although most officers do not attend the national conferences, many do go to the state-level association meetings. Many of these existing networks of public officials include fostering the cooperation and exchange of information among law enforcement agencies in their mission statements, and they commonly look for mutually beneficial partnerships. The State and Provincial Police division of IACP, for example, operates a listserv where information is exchanged among the 49 state police departments and the Canadian provinces. Having NLECTC do a better job of periodically seeking out the appropriate individuals within these organizations and asking if they are willing to pass on information or opportunities available through NLECTC would go a long way toward improving awareness of the NLECTC program.

Further Study

As noted, focus groups and interviews are intended primarily to surface needs and issues, not to assess their prevalence statistically. Even in studies such as this one, in which we interviewed representatives from a comparatively large number of agencies and responses were highly consistent, any assessments of prevalence must be considered preliminary. Consequently, we believe the results of this study can help inform the development of more targeted questions on upcoming survey studies asking agencies about technology prevalence and technology needs, as well as how both the federal government and technology providers could best support departments (for example, through various options for technology acquisition business models). The results would provide greater levels of specificity and granularity as to agencies' technology needs, subdivided by agency size and focus.

Conclusions

NIJ, and its NLECTC system, has the charge and ability to plug technology gaps, provide expert advice, and improve knowledge dissemination among the country's plethora of criminal justice departments. The initial characterization of agencies' current information technology needs, as well as ways to improve NIJ and NLECTC's outreach efforts, is intended to assist NIJ and NLECTC in meeting these objectives.

We emphasize that the results of this study, centered on focus groups, are intended to be a first step in gaining better awareness of agencies' technology needs. Subsequent survey studies, and repeated rounds of focus groups, surveys, and expert advisory panels, will be needed to gain more detailed awareness of what agencies' needs for technology and NIJ support are, as well as track how those needs are changing over time.

Current NIJ Outreach Processes

NIJ has several mechanisms that can serve both to distribute information to practitioners and to receive input regarding the most pressing needs toward which it should allocate resources. All of these processes are currently within the NLECTC system, which was designed to focus on a number of law enforcement and criminal justice subject areas so that gaps can be identified and research thrusts can be allocated appropriately at the federal level.

Center System

NLECTC—a free resource created in 1994 and designed to address the technology needs of law enforcement, corrections, and criminal justice agencies—is central to the NIJ's efforts to assist state and local criminal justice communities. As Figure A.1 shows, NLECTC comprises four regional centers that cater to specific constituencies, plus eight CoEs with functional expertise. These centers are all NIJ grantees or awardees and, thus, serve specific NIJ submissions that involve both outreach to the practitioners that make up NIJ's customer base and providing those practitioners with resources to interface with NLECTC and access the research, evaluation, and assistance performed within the center system.

JUSTNET

Information on specific centers and contact information to request assistance is available via JUSTNET, the Justice Technology Information Network. This website is NLECTC's public face and a repository of news, research, and information about law enforcement and criminal justice technology. It is used to disseminate knowledge to the practitioner community and is the easiest and fastest way to obtain information about the NLECTC system and any research done therein.

TechBeat

NLECTC's flagship publication is a newsmagazine titled *TechBeat* (see Figure A.2). Issued quarterly, it is available via hard copy or electronic subscription at no cost. *TechBeat* is the primary means by which NLECTC keeps practitioners updated with research, technologies, and standards being developed within the NLECTC system.

Figure A.1
NLECTC Organization

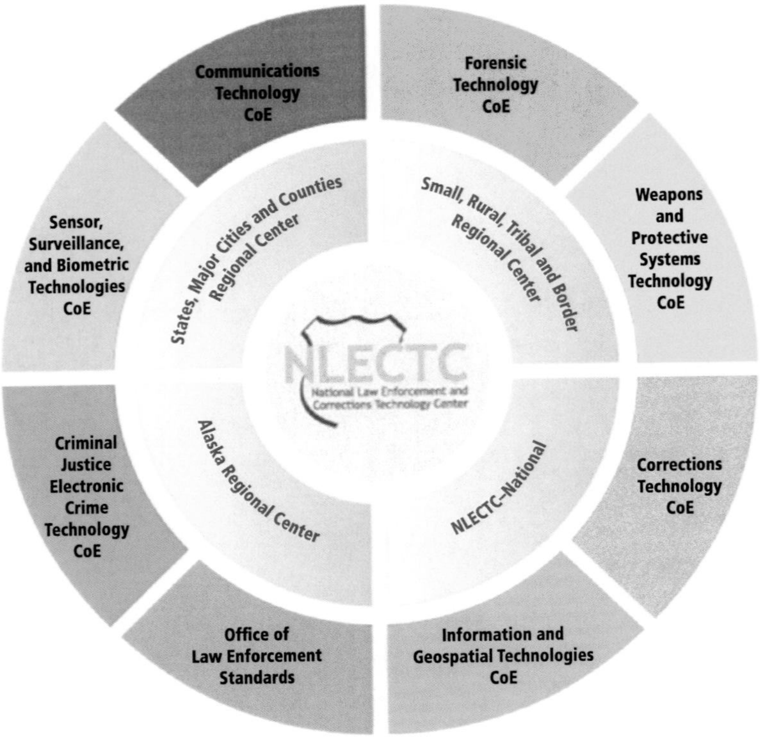

SOURCE: National Law Enforcement and Corrections Technology Center (NLECTC)–National,
a program of the National Institute of Justice. Used with permission.
RAND TR1165-A.1

Technology Working Groups

NIJ funds research, testing, and evaluation efforts through a targeted grant solicitation process. Each solicitation falls under one of 18 technology investment portfolios: aviation, biometrics, body armor, communications, community corrections, DNA forensics, electronic crime, explosive device defeat, general (non-DNA) forensics, geospatial technologies, information-led policing and courts technologies, institutional corrections, less-lethal technologies, operations research/modeling and simulation, officer safety and protective technologies, pursuit management, school safety, and sensors and surveillance (National Institute of Justice, 2010). In order to determine which "high-priority needs" arise from each portfolio, NIJ has set up a series of TWGs composed of approximately 20 practitioners with subject-matter expertise in that area. Each CoE runs the TWGs for its respective portfolios. The RAND IGT CoE's responsibilities include support of four portfolios: information-led policing, modeling and simulation, operations research, and geospatial technologies. This is the first step of the process that NIJ has in place to elicit input and needs from the practitioner community when prioritizing its grant solicitation funds. The second step involves review of the TWG recommendations by the Law Enforcement and Corrections Technology Advisory Council, an advisory body of 35–40 criminal justice practitioners that meets once

Figure A.2
TechBeat Online Cover

SOURCE: National Law Enforcement and Corrections Technology Center
(NLECTC)–National, a program of the National Institute of Justice. Used with permission.
RAND *TR1165-A.2*

a year. This body produces an annual report that includes two tiers of technology priorities: a
"Top 10 Needs and Requirements" list and six "Additional Priorities" (Law Enforcement and
Corrections Technology Advisory Council, 2010).

References

Collins, Pamela, et al., *Law Enforcement Technology—Are Small and Rural Agencies Equipped and Trained?* Washington, D.C.: National Institute of Justice Research for Practice Report NCJ 204609, June 2004.

Groups Plus, Inc., *Frequently Asked Questions About Focus Groups* web page, 2008. As of October 4, 2012: http://www.groupsplus.com/pages/faq.htm

Grudens-Schuck, Nancy, Beverlyn Lundy Allen, and Kathlene Larson, *Focus Group Fundamentals*, Ames, Iowa: Iowa State University Extension, Methodology Brief PM-1969B, May 2004. As of October 4, 2012: http://www.extension.iastate.edu/publications/pm1969b.pdf

Hamilton, Alexander, "Federalist 17," *The Federalist Papers*, Independent Journal, December 1787.

Integrated Justice Information Systems Institute, *Programs* web page, 2010. As of September 17, 2012: http://www.ijis.org/_programs/Programs.html

International Association of Chiefs of Police, *CAD/RMS* web page, 2012. As of September 17, 2012: http://www.theiacp.org/Technology/OperationalTechnologies/CADRMS/tabid/831/Default.aspx

Koper, Christopher S., et al., *Law Enforcement Technology Needs Assessment: Future Technologies to Address the Operational Needs of Law Enforcement*, Washington, D.C.: Police Executive Research Forum, January 16, 2009.

JUSTNET, the Justice Technology Information Network, *About NLECTC* web page, undated. As of October 17, 2012: https://www.justnet.org/About_NLECTC.html

Law Enforcement and Corrections Technology Advisory Council, *2010 Annual Report*, National Law Enforcement and Corrections Technology Center, 2010. As of October 4, 2012: https://www.justnet.org/pdf/LECTAC-2010-Report.pdf

National Information Exchange Model Program Management Office, home page, 2012. As of September 17, 2012: https://www.niem.gov/Pages/default.aspx

National Institute of Justice, Office of Justice Programs, *High Priority Criminal Justice Technology Needs*, U.S. Department of Justice, 2010. As of October 4, 2012: https://www.ncjrs.gov/pdffiles1/nij/230391.pdf

National Law Enforcement and Corrections Technology Center, homepage, undated. As of October 25, 2012: http://www.justnet.org

National Oceanic and Atmospheric Administration Coastal Services Center, *Introduction to Conducting Focus Groups*, Charleston, S.C., 2009. As of October 4, 2012: http://www.csc.noaa.gov/focus_groups/

Reaves, Brian, *Local Police Departments, 2007*, Washington, D.C.: U.S. Department of Justice, Bureau of Justice Statistics, 2010.

———, *Census of State and Local Law Enforcement Agencies, 2008*, U.S. Department of Justice, Bureau of Justice Statistics, 2011.

Schwabe, William, Lois M. Davis, and Brian A. Jackson, *Challenges and Choices for Crime Fighting Technology: Federal Support of State and Local Law Enforcement*, Santa Monica, Calif.: RAND Corporation MR-1349-OSTP/NIJ, 2001. As of October 24, 2012:
http://www.rand.org/pubs/monograph_reports/MR1349.html

U.S. Department of Justice, Office of Justice Programs, *Global Justice Information Sharing Initiative* web page, 2012. As of September 17, 2012:
http://www.it.ojp.gov/global

TechBeat, Winter 2011 archived issue web page, undated. As of October 17, 2012:
https://www.justnet.org/InteractiveTechBeat/

Zhang, Yan, and Barbara M. Wildemuth, "Qualitative Analysis of Content," *Applications of Social Research Methods to Questions in Information and Library*, Santa Barbara, Calif.: Libraries Unlimited, 2009.